1000
REASONS
TO BE
HAPPY

1000
REASONS
TO BE
HAPPY

David Baird

MQP

Contents

Introduction

Whatever the reasons:
  That the bills are paid,
  That the fish are biting,
  That the clock is on time,
  That the sea comes to shore,
  That the milk hasn't curdled,
  That the can-can was invented,
  That it's your birthday tomorrow,
  Or that there are pancakes at teatime,
Happiness comes in all shapes
  and forms,
And a little bit of happiness does
  everyone a whole lot of good.

The world can at times seem dark and filled with foreboding. Sometimes our happiness can become threatened by the events that surround us. But listen up. Happiness breeds happiness.

That's a fact that mustn't be ignored, and if we truly want a happier, friendlier, more caring, and fairer world, then it is up to each and every one of us to start living happier lives now. We decide and we make it happen.

So to get things started, here are a thousand reasons I can think of to boot up my happy drive.

You may not agree with them all, or you may have a thousand of your own . . . the important thing is to start putting positive thoughts into action. So come on . . . *get up . . . get happy!*

Work and Creativity

1

*Happiness
is an in-tray
that's out.*

The more **interests**
you **have**, the more
chances of
happiness you **have**.

Here's a **happy** thought—extraordinary people can **never** be replaced by machines.

Having nice workmates is truly a reason to be very happy.

Don't **minimize** your contribution. Be happy to **know** that **any** productive work or activity you undertake makes a positive **change** to this world.

For the artist, designer, hairdresser, or house painter, happiness is in the final look.

"*A man's work is rather the needful supplement to himself than the outcome of it.*"

MAX BEERBOHM

Happiness is **enjoying** your achievements, no matter **how** small.

Think happy thoughts — all achievement begins with an idea.

Creativity is a natural method of expressing our enthusiasm for life and being happy.

Teaching that happiness is dependent solely upon success is like saying that virtue is the domain of those who preach falsehood.

One source of happiness is **knowing** we are in the **right place** at the **right time** to facilitate our own growth.

You don't have to make hard work of being happy. Sit back and relax into it.

Taking complete personal responsibility is a reason to be happy.

Domestic chores are rather like a temperamental partner. We rarely get much love back, but we're happy to stick at it.

Happiness is the hum of busy concentration in a classroom, like bees in a hive— everything smacks of honey.

The bandages on my fingers and the sweat on my brow are well worth it for the satisfaction of a task well completed.

Our **minds** are always at the level we **believe** ourselves to be at. Many a mailroom clerk **could** run the company if he or she were only **asked**.

"Honest labor bears a lovely face."

THOMAS DEKKER

The happiest result is the one that you worked hard for.

After the rigors of a long day the happiest thing to come home to is the grace of tenderness.

"One of the saddest things is that the only thing a man can do for eight hours a day, day after day, is work. You can't eat eight hours a day nor drink for eight hours a day nor make love for eight hours."

WILLIAM FAULKNER

"Originality and the feeling of one's own dignity are achieved only through work and struggle."

FYODOR DOSTOEVSKY

Happiness is
remembering passes,
exams or driving tests.

Being **part** of a **team**
is **better** than being a
solo contender.

*Happiness is entering into
any endeavor determined
to play your very best.*

Happiness is having a handful of **teachers**, **coaches**, or **guides** who **lead** through **inspiration**.

Happiness is any kind of surprises but bad ones.

Happiness is the power of being organized.

Anything that **exercises** the **imagination** in a **positive** way is a **source** of **happiness**.

**Projects
that reach
their target and
give you a sense
of achievement
are reasons
to be happy.**

"When work is a pleasure, life is a joy!"

MAXIM GORKY

Sustained happiness can
be attained through the
practice of making simple,
immediate decisions.

**Happiness is the ability
to completely lose yourself
in a task or hobby.**

Happiness is being able to rely upon oneself and not having to depend upon others.

Happiness is believing in yourself and knowing you have only equals.

Justice done is happiness won.

Happiness lies in truth. How can we possibly hope to be happy if we never know if what we're talking about, saying, or being told is true or not?

Happiness is being **brave enough** to just **do** what it is that you do **best**.

Happiness comes to those with no longing to do those things for which they have no ability.

A person's worth consists in what they are and not in what they have.

Happiness is
being positive.
Positive **thoughts** engender
positive **feelings** that
engender positive **actions.**

Happy is the person who has found continuity of purpose.

Having **clear**, **achievable**, **meaningful goals** in life is a strong **key** to **unlocking personal** happiness.

Know that **riches,** **mediocrity,** and **poverty** begin in the **mind.** A **happy mind** is the key to a **happy life.**

Having good ideas when you need them the most certainly brings happiness.

Happiness is a job— a job completed.

Life has taught me to be happy with the thought that I am just as important as anybody else.

I am **happier** when I have **precisely defined objectives**.

People who answer their telephones make me happy.

We can all experience true success—it is mirrored in how we get along with others.

I know that cooperation promotes happiness.

As much as I would **love** to experience **lots and lots** of money, I **know** that money **can't** buy happiness— I'm **happy** as I **am**.

Happiness is the ability to lose yourself in concentration on a task or hobby.

I am happy to know that even masters had to take the first step.

Positive thinking evokes more energy, more initiative, and more happiness.

Success is only a part of happiness and should never come at the expense of sacrificing all the other elements necessary for true happiness.

Each of us is **born** with **great potential** and it is up to **each** of us to **reach** it. Happiness **is** reaching that potential.

Happiness is being able to determine your life's direction.

Happiness is a clear mind. One can see all the choices and deal with anything.

Some become separated by the deep chasms of their differences while others cross to meet each other half way on bridges of happiness.

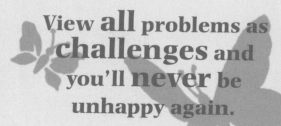

View **all** problems as **challenges** and you'll **never** be unhappy again.

**Happiness
is about trying.
Failure?
Not trying is
far worse than
failure.**

When we are happy to accept that things sometimes can and do go wrong, then our failures become our teachers and not our jailers.

When we are **determined**, we may experience **delay**, but never **defeat**. That's a **happy** notion.

One of the happier sounds I know is the silent approach of a deadline when I am ready to meet it.

Invest in tomorrow's happiness by doing good work today.

Happiness is being given the opportunity for fresh starts— even if they come to us in less happy disguises.

The world is happier now that telex machines have all but disappeared. So much quieter.

If happiness only comes with knowledge, then why is so much enjoyment gained from useless knowledge?

If you are going to seek happiness through visual art, you must be prepared to use your vision.

The predictable is far from exciting. I'd rather have the happiness provided by a strange dream any time.

Sometimes the greatest happiness of all is the bliss of being ignorant of all the facts.

There is **happiness** sometimes in **finding out** that we were **wrong**, **even** when we were **certain** we were **right**.

Optimism is something to look forward to. Who would be happy to see a world in every grain of sand?

Happiness is living with the **confidence** that with **time** and **patience** one can usually figure things out.

There's happiness in the well-earned break as well as the job well done.

*Anything that
I have created for
myself gives me great
happiness.*

**Unhappy is anyone
who cannot find some
pleasure at the tenacity of
cartoon characters.**

Theaters make me **happy,** and **so** do their **audiences**: the stubborn attempts of mankind to **rediscover** something of being **human together** through the medium of **play**.

A well-made collage is a happy sight: somehow, like life, bringing all the disparate pieces together into some larger coherent whole!

Happiness is what the farmer feels who after hard toil sees the fruits of his labor.

Happiness is coming to a level of understanding of those things which before we were clueless about.

Who does not feel happiness when they discover the job they wanted so much has been offered to them?

"I like work: It fascinates me. I can sit and look at it for hours. I love to keep it by me: The idea of getting rid of it nearly breaks my heart."

JEROME K. JEROME

Happiness is feeling you are in control of your life.

Some of the greatest happiness I have seen was expressed by people who had satisfactorily completed their crossword puzzles!

No music composed, either ancient or modern, is not capable of stimulating in me some form of happy reaction.

Happiness can be found in the simple pleasures of wordplay and puns. A sign perhaps of a misspelt youth!

The imagination of a good author is always cause for happiness to their readers and audiences.

Happy people can get as much enjoyment from the **wrappers** as they do from the **chocolates**.

Writing is a truly stimulating and freeing enterprise that brings much happiness to the writer and reader alike.

Poetry that stands the test of time will bring happiness over and over again, no matter how often we read it.

Happy people are those who have learned to let go.

That moment when you begin to write a story and the uncertainty and the excitement it brings is the most terrifyingly happy moment I know.

Mellow moods of sultry verse make for happy emotions.

Happiness is discovering **snow angels** in unexpected places.

Happiness is the spiral staircase that leads to my imagination.

Happiness is theirs who, instead of drowning in a sea of cables, know exactly which cord leads to which socket.

Happiness is knowing that my contributions are valued.

The moment we decide to be happy we open the secret door through which we can discover the power to create and live the life we want.

There are no shortcuts to creativity. You plant the seed, it germinates and grows. Then, with nourishment and loving care, you can harvest the crop. So too with lifelong happiness.

Happiness is giving as much as I can to everything I do.

It makes me extremely
happy that every time
I expect less I always
seem to get more.

The fleeting artistry of
blowing bubbles brings
sheer pleasure to all
who observe them.

I am always happier knowing that I am easily pleased.

I am happier to acknowledge that things will go wrong, rather than the unhappy alternative of going through life saying nothing and doing nothing.

One of the most important things in the happiness equation is understanding that we are all in negotiation with life and that we must not compromise our own happiness.

As you come to understand the reasons for things, the happier you become.

Happiness is the winning goal.

2

Food and Familiar Places

Good food not only feeds but brings happiness on many levels.

Happiness is bobbing for apples.

"Happiness: a good bank account, a good cook, and a good digestion."

JEAN-JACQUES ROUSSEAU

My greatest happiness is made up of many little happinesses— fistfuls of colored jelly beans.

Saturday sandwiches crammed with all the best fillings are a happy repast.

Slippers that were meant to be taken seriously are a great source of happiness and mirth.

A summer recipe for happiness is cucumber sandwiches, crusts off, served on the veranda.

Olives with everything—black ones, green ones, stuffed ones—fill me with happy thoughts of the Mediterranean.

Waking in a room that is bathed in glorious sunlight is sure to put me in a happy state of mind.

I feel **safe** in the **knowledge** that there is **no** one recipe for happiness.

Tooth fairy payouts have always managed to raise a smile, even if it has a few gaps in it!

Happiness is biting into a jelly-filled donut.

Picnics on the riverbank in loving memory of old Mr. Toad. He'd be happy to know we enjoy that.

A **homemade** meal simmering on the range, **wafting** its presence throughout each room, every floor of the house, and halfway through the neighborhood, is a **recipe** for **happiness**.

Breakfast can be a wonderful time of the day to dine out, but it can be doubly good if you take someone with you.

Happiness is the **welcoming** sound of my **key** as it turns in the **lock**.

"You are a king by your own fireside, as much as any monarch in his throne."

CERVANTES

If my nose has one good reason to feel happy, it would have to be the welcome aroma of freshly brewed coffee.

I know that fragrant tea makes many people very happy; it's just not my cup of tea.

It is said that **passion** often leads to **upset**, but when a person is able to **master** and **control** their passions happiness can be **having** your **cake** and **eating** it.

"The discovery of a new **dish** does **more** for human happiness than the discovery of a new **star**."

ANTHELME BRILLAT-SAVARIN

Macaroni and cheese— one of my favorite recipes for happiness.

Happiness is discovering that there are always more reasons to get up in the morning than there are for not doing so.

Happiness is a bowl of fluffy mashed potatoes for one, for another plump rice, for me— marshmallows.

Desserts of almost any kind are happiness.

Happiness is slicing my own home-grown, home-watered, home-sown, and home-cropped tomatoes.

I love to cook but, better still, adore having someone cook for me.

The **closest** thing to love is **chocolate**. The closest thing to **true** love is **dark** chocolate.

Happiness is deciding on the design of your birthday cake.

Here's a **happy** thought: **Tennis** was invented to **coincide** with the **strawberry** season.

Happiness is a penny in my share of the pudding.

Some cause for happiness is that one can usually, but not without effort, find the missing sock.

A pyramid of homemade fudge is a happy sight.

Scoop upon scoop of ice cream makes Jack a happy lad.

Happiness is the freedom to experiment with different flavors.

Lying out in my hammock
makes me blissfully happy.

Slicing up cool
mangoes on warm
summer mornings
makes me happy.

The perfume of night-scented
jasmine fills my imagination
with happiness.

Happiness is a mug of hot cocoa on a cold winter evening, beside the fire.

Happiness is about feeling safe.

Happiness is rediscovering the familiar roads that lead us back to happy memories of our homelife.

Happiness is the quest for anything excellent, especially pizza or pasta . . . curry . . . kabobs.

There's happiness in the simple design and delicate texture of a croissant.

The happy designs on my pajamas when I view them hanging on the bathroom door make me laugh.

I am happy that I have the freedom of self-expression to paint my walls and hang my curtains as I wish.

Happiness is modeling
that **last** scrap of dough
into a **work** of pastry **art**.

*Who is not happy to
discover the immense value
of being able to hang a
picture straight?*

Happiness is the **perfume** of
clean laundry brought in
from **blowing** in the **wind**.

Moments of quiet reflection in my sun-filled kitchen are little havens of happiness.

There's happiness in trying to **unpick** the **unspoken** history of an antique quilt.

One of the **simplest** methods of **stirring** my **soul** is to **catch** a **whiff** of baking bread.

Listening to my chatty petunias fills me with happy thoughts.

Happiness is the first mouthful of new-season fruit straight from the orchard.

Being **blanketed** in the feather **softness** of an eiderdown is **bliss**.

Happiness is admiring the earth's bounty at a well-stocked market.

For the chef, happiness is about pleasing others.

Afternoon tea laid out in the shade of the summer sun is a recipe for happiness.

Watching children armed with imagination and colored sprinkles decorating a tray of cupcakes is reason to be happy.

Happiness is scraping out the mixing bowl.

Here's a happy thought—
fortune cookies that
come true.

Dreaming up menus
for fantastic feasts
is a happy pastime.

The **belief** that **anything** is possible is a **recipe** for happiness.

Happiness on a hot day? Iced tea please!

A well-stocked dessert tray, strategically placed, makes for a happy diner.

Happiness is the sound of the Sunday morning newspaper being delivered.

Then there is the **clatter** of **teacups** that **heralds** the **happy** thought of breakfast in **bed**.

The hallos that are sung by summer flowers as they greet me year after year makes me a happy person.

Having found sunshine in so many places, I can have sunshine at any moment, whenever I like.

Coming home with **baskets** of **summer berries** has me **trembling** with happy anticipation of the **feast** that is to come.

A happy person never has anything other than a sense of good things to come in the days ahead.

Homemade dinners, the loving sounds of them being prepared, and of course the tantalizing aromas that tickle the taste buds are reasons enough to be happy.

Designing for yourself a **quiet** life where **true** joy can dwell is **sure** to make you happy.

Happiness is about acceptance.

When we learn to celebrate common, everyday occurrences then all of life becomes something to be savored.

The echo of the church bell on a midsummer's evening, not pressuring me to come but reassuring me that it's there.

A mirror free from toothpaste spatters reveals a happy face.

The company of my footsteps as I walk along in the dark comforts me.

A restful night's sleep on a comfortable bed brings me happiness beyond compare.

Lawns that don't turn brown bring me as much happiness as diamonds or gingerbread.

Public footpaths and other **rights of way** are there to make **everybody** happy.

A mosquito-free zone is a heaven-sent gift— mosquitoes, you see, make me very unhappy.

Happy time is spent sweeping the pathway and greeting passers-by.

Happiness is my neighbor, leaving fresh bread and a carton of milk to welcome me home from my travels.

It is a happy life when I am confident that my cherished pets are in the caring hands of my neighbor when I am abroad.

There's happiness with every bunch of flowers that colors the furniture surfaces.

Happiness is the disappearance of a nagging headache, replaced by that joyful sense of a new beginning.

Catching a few phrases of a song being sung, or live music being played through an open window as I pass by, always lifts my spirits.

A **cluttered** life is **distracting** to me. It signifies things left undone or unfinished. It places life on hold. **Tidiness** to me is **liberating**.

Happiness is finding the **stillness** of the **day** and the **peace** of the **night**.

I'm happy with the fizz
of ice-cold lemonade
beneath my nose.

*Happiness is
watching my
soufflé rise.*

Slam the dishwasher
door closed with a
happy sigh of relief.

The regular rhythm of the to-ing and fro-ing of quiet domesticity makes me happy.

Happiness is in the jars of jelly from the farm shop with their promise of happy eating.

The smell of freshly squeezed lemon juice makes me happy.

Feet up, body sunk into the sofa, TV on—I'm happy.

Happiness is the peace of mind that documents are stored safely.

Happiness is clearing the junk to the charity store.

The cathartic qualities of spring cleaning make for a happy home.

Much **happiness** is to be **gained** from the **simple addition** to one's life of a reliable **alarm** clock.

Recycling puts happiness back into circulation.

Is there a pair of shoes anywhere at any price that can match the happy comfort of bare feet?

"A home is not a mere transient shelter: Its essence lies in its permanence, in its capacity for accretion and solidification, in its quality of representing, in all its details, the personalities of the people who live in it."

H. L. MENCKEN

Happiness is being able to find a safety pin when your button pops off and you're in a hurry.

Happiness is crunching ice cubes on hot summer days.

The happiest **statement** I can think of is the statement from the **bank** that tells you you're **clear** of **debt**.

Stains are happiest when they're gone.

"Of the good things given
    Between man and woman,
I say that a neighbor
    True and loving in heart,
To neighbor is a joy beyond
    All things else."

PINDAR

Happiness comes
through feeling at peace.

3

My World

That I am proud just to be me is my happiest discovery.

We are happy when we are admired **without** seeking admiration, when we are praised **without** seeking praise.

When you have control over your thoughts, you have control over your life. What better reason for being happy?

"Find ecstasy in life; the mere sense of living is joy enough."

EMILY DICKINSON

My **soul** is like a **kite** and the **less** tightly I hold the string the **freer** it is to **soar.**

Things that don't involve me jumping out of airplanes make me happy.

Great happiness is to be found when we can generate for ourselves a state of calmness, relaxation, and peace while being fully awake and fully aware.

I am happy in the knowledge that I am **entitled** to my own **opinion**, and happier still to **see** my opinion **published** as a letter in the newspaper.

I still like finding a penny and making a wish.

I love it when something is so good that it exceeds description.

Receiving a **thank you** when I have put **myself** out to **help** makes me happy.

My happiness gives me the power
to deal with anything in life.

My **vision** of heaven
is where **happiness**
is not only **infinite**
but **eternal**.

**Happiness is sliding
through the changing
colors of a kaleidoscope.**

Happiness is the arrival of your first bike.

"Even if happiness forgets you a little bit, never completely forget about it."

JACQUES PRÉVERT

Happiness is the **taste** of **freedom** when you learn to ride a bike.

"A string of excited, fugitive, miscellaneous pleasures is not happiness; happiness resides in imaginative reflection and judgment, when the picture of one's life, or of human life, as it truly has been or is, satisfies the will, and is gladly accepted."

GEORGE SANTAYANA

I will be happiest never finding out why the universe exists.

The best remedy for any wrongs is to move on and forget them. Only this way can one be happy.

I am always happy to find a new book by a favorite author.

Life has granted me the **discovery** that unhappiness is a **sea** of **delusions** from which only **we** can **rescue** ourselves.

A happy sound is that of a muffled sneeze and the giggles that follow it amid the quiet hush of a library.

Time has helped me to come to appreciate the transient nature of some of the things that bring happiness into my life.

I believe that my being happy is a step toward creating a happier world.

Happiness is knowing and accepting that my personal quest for happiness is not self-centered or unfair.

Does happiness lay in riches?
The fewer wants we have in
life the greater our
possessions become.

*I am happy that
I am confident.*

Days when I wake **filled** with
optimism and **boundless
energy** make me **very** happy.

The feeling of happiness I enjoy the most is the one I get when I make people around me happy.

I am **happy** because there's no **better time** to be happy than **right now.**

Happiness comes through retaining a sense of curiosity throughout one's entire life.

I am **happy** because my life is **filled** with **challenges**, therefore I can **never** be bored.

I am happy to have learned that in the wisdom of uncertainty lies the freedom from our past, and the freedom from the known.

Since allowing happiness into my life, I worry less and my rest is free from anxiety.

*I am happy that if
I touch one thing
with deep awareness,
I touch everything.*

I am happier to spend **each**
and **every new moment**
in wisdom, understanding,
and love — **not** in fear, anger,
jealousy, guilt, or regret.

I love having something happy to remember.

I love **candles**, and the way they make the **shadows** dance **merrily** around the room at night.

Happiness is the **knowledge** that I can **not** change **everything,** but that **those** things that **I can** change for the better, **I will**.

I am happy that tomorrow is another day.

I take great satisfaction from things that take my mind off everything.

Bookmarks that journey through books with me are happy companions.

"The reason angels can fly is that they take themselves so lightly."

G. K. CHESTERTON

I don't fear the opinion of others. I am happy to hear it, whatever it is.

I **no longer** feel **envy** toward **any other** human being. I am **happy just** to be **me**.

I have found happiness by taking steps to ensure that my life contains the prerequisites for happiness and by systematically removing as many of the causes of unhappiness as possible.

I am only human, and
all humans, even when
we do the best we can,
still make mistakes.
I don't need to punish
myself with unhappiness.

The world I live in is the way I perceive it. I am happy to say that I think that it is still filled with great promise.

I am happiest just being myself.

Our social status, the state of our health, the color of our skin, have little to do with finding and keeping happiness in our life. Avoiding the hard knocks and tricks of fate that life deals to us are all excellent reasons for happiness.

141

Imagine your **life** as a **turbulent ocean**. The moment you **choose** to let happiness **into** your life, the **waters** calm down and become as **still** as a **mirror**.

I am happy to thank those people who have dedicated their lives to making me laugh.

Being within earshot of the drama suggested by foghorns on a foggy day fills me with happy thoughts.

Seeing girls with shocking pink hair and audaciously loud, bright-colored nails makes me happy.

Whatever your worries, know this:
There is no one out there who is
plotting your unhappiness.
That's reason to be happy.

Here's a happy thought:
A **smile** is a **curve**
that sets **everything**
straight.

Feeling accepted by my peers is an important reason to feel happy.

Unexpected **encounters** with **strangers** who **reveal** a **new** world to me **satisfy** my happy **curiosity**.

The discovery of a kindred spirit is a gateway to happiness.

Realizing **how** fortunate I am in the **greater** scheme of things gives me **reasons** to **celebrate** every day!

"To be stupid, selfish, and have good health are three requirements for happiness, though if stupidity is lacking, all is lost."

GUSTAVE FLAUBERT

Sometimes, to **ensure** you are happy about the **priorities** in your life, it's good to list **ten** things—things that are **capable** of bringing you **continual** happiness.

The first happy moment will come the instant we discover that it is our choice to be happy. Happiness is a great empowerer.

Being able to laugh at ourselves is a reason to be happy.

Happiness is seeing life and our part in it as an enormous bundle of great possibilities.

Happiness is discovering the serenity that lies within all of us.

"To the mind that is still,
the whole universe surrenders."

LAO TZU

When you are **able** to
achieve and maintain
inner peace, happiness
knows **no bounds**.

**Happiness is being freed from
the chains of a rigid mindset.**

Happiness is **living** for **each** and **every** moment.

Here's a happy thought: **no one** can be happy who does not **think** themselves to be so.

Happiness is finding that the last lemon on the tree isn't you.

Happiness is doing what you've been meaning to do.

Happiness is trying new things for the first time just for the fun of it. Fun does us good.

Deciphering hieroglyphics, now that makes me happy.

Shedding those unwanted pounds makes me happy.

Happiness is a **pair** of **new** shoes in their tissue wrapping, **waiting** to be worn.

Happiness is running with freedom.

I'm well.
My heart beats.
I'm happy!

My happy thought is that we are all riding this world through space.

What a happy moment of freedom when I shed my winter coat to the summer warmth.

"There are two ways of spreading light; to be the candle or the mirror that reflects it."

EDITH WHARTON

If I could **choose** a happy place to live, it might be the **wonderful, peaceful world** that exists **inside** snow shakers.

What is my secret of happiness? I live as simply as I can. With this, a person never grows old.

I am as happy to accept that not all problems have solutions as I am happy to accept that almost all problems do have solutions.

"If my **heart** can become **pure** and **simple** like that of a **child**, I think there probably can be no greater happiness than this."

KITARO NISHIDA

Procrastination sometimes makes me happy.

Things that make me happy? Maraschino cherries, getting a parking spot, inspiring lyrics, blowing dandelion clocks.

Knowing exactly what I want frees me from the unhappiness of uncertainty.

Knowing we made the right decision is the greatest cause for happiness for most of us.

Whenever today seems just too much to bear, I find happiness in the knowledge that tomorrow will soon come with the hope of a reprieve.

"Happiness is like a butterfly, which, when you pursue it is always beyond your grasp, but which, when you sit down may alight upon you."

NATHANIEL HAWTHORNE

I am always made happy by the fact that someone, somewhere invented the musical saw. Now that had to be a happy person.

I am happy that, despite daily discoveries in mathematics, two and two still make four.

People who make me happy include clowns, jugglers, stilt walkers, and all circus folk and show people who keep at it, no matter what.

So what if we have doubts about ourselves and our abilities—we're wiser than the real fanatics and complete fools who are always certain of themselves. I'm happy not to be like that!

I am happy to convince myself and others that auctions are a form of recycling.

I am happiest when things are clean— including myself.

I have recognized, after years of traveling this world, that in truth very little is needed by any person to make a happy life. If it were not so the obituaries would outsize the news.

I am happy having happy thoughts, such as: Imagine the possibilities if all could feel happy.

I am happy each **summer** that, **despite** being around at the time of **Christ, sandals** are **still** fashionable today.

Nothing except nature can compare with the value of movies. For the price of a couple of dollars, you can enter a world that cost $70 million to make. Now that makes me very happy indeed.

Any kind of a win is a win-win
situation if it makes you happy.

*Music that defines
a period, whether
Baroque or 1980s pop,
makes me happy.*

**Happiness is a familiar movie
I can watch time and time again.**

Anything one can accomplish oneself despite the odds is good reason for happiness.

Happiness can come through the **silky** feel of **hair** to the **touch**.

Happy nights include mankind's tribute to meteor showers— grand firework displays!

The **ticking** of a **clock** makes me **happier** than when they **tock**.

People on the **whole** seem **infinitely** happier when the dentist's **drill** they can **hear** is in someone **else's** mouth.

A great long, gaping yawn makes me happy, particularly when observed coming from a hippopotamus or a politician.

Happiness need not depend upon life's lotteries; it can be as simple as a pair of well-loved shoes.

Happiness is being able to climb off life's ladder so that nobody is above or below you.

Happiness comes the first time we find the **courage** within ourselves to stick up for what is **right**, and the **ability** to say what we **truly** feel.

Happiness is discovering the **forgiveness** that lies locked in your heart.

Happiness comes when we surrender ourselves to the anticipation of something good or exciting.

The first time for everything is a source of happiness.

Happiness is a few well-chosen words offered at the right time.

I am always happier knowing that I am easily pleased and spoiled for choice.

Happiness is a special gift from someone you love.

Just **knowing** where things are is **cause** for **great** jubilation in my life.

Vases of fresh cut flowers are like happy, smiling faces greeting you when you enter the room.

Happiness is finding a feather to place in your hair.

Happiness is good-night kisses and long walks home.

Who has not abandoned themselves to the happy escape that reading provides?

Happiness is **rediscovering** something that was **uplifting** or **inspiring** the **first** time round, and it having the **same** effect **again**.

Happiness is about never allowing my own judgment to cloud the water or disturb me.

I am happy that
I understand the true
value of things.
Life has taught me that
I don't need to wait
for the well to run dry
in order to know the
worth of water.

Enjoying
the Good
Times

Lazy days and a swimming pool are a happy combination.

Beaches where the large and the hairy, the great and the good, are made to feel welcome too are genuine cause for happiness.

Make a happy diary by creating memorable time in your itinerary each week.

Visits to happy zoos where they take care of the animals make me happy.

Watching kids laughing for hours on a trampoline is a happy sight.

A bucket of popcorn and a matinee at the local cinema is happiness personified.

A championship tournament of tiddlywinks can raise anyone's spirit, anytime, anywhere.

"If you can spend a perfectly useless afternoon in a perfectly useless manner, you have learned how to live."

LIN YUTANG

Participating in workshops and courses in the arts and crafts can provide the happiness of returning home with your handmade vase or the violin that you carved for your daughter.

Happiness is visiting places where history was made.

Happy times are expeditions to pick plump summer fruits.

Nobody welcomes being **pushed** around, but being **thrown about** by the **waves** . . . ah, well . . . that's a **different** matter.

A happy life is the result of making every day a significant day.

Swimming underwater for as **long** as I can and the happy intake of **breath** as I break the surface makes me feel alive.

People who are involved in chess games in public parks always look peaceful and happy.

People who ice-skate for the very first time may not look too happy, but they are.

"Sit quietly, doing **nothing**, spring **comes**, and the grass **grows** by itself."

ZEN SAYING

Happy evenings spent in town, taking in a show are blissful.

Tinkering seems to be what I was **born** for. I'm happy to do that.

What could make anyone happier than having ice-cream sundaes at around midnight with friends?

I'm happy that kite flying hasn't been banned and that yo-yos still exist.

Happiness is closing time and opening time.

Aren't we all happy that advertising hasn't found its way into novels!

I'm happy that one can **still** go out and hear a **song** in the **street**.

Everybody's happy that musicals never seem dated.

Happiness is that moment between closing my book at night, switching out the light, and turning my face to the pillow.

I'm happy to see bicycles on city roads and scooters and rollerblades on city sidewalks.

I'm happy to sing out the praises of my favorite musicians.

Heaven is soaking **tired** feet in **warm** water.

The happy whoosh of bathwater running thrills me to the core. I close my eyes and I'm by a jungle waterfall.

Books are like holidays; between their covers lie entire worlds. Whoever thinks that time travel is impossible has never immersed themselves in a good book.

Shhh! Happiness is reading a book without interruption.

I am happy with my ability to take myself out of myself with a good movie.

What could be more **stimulating** than **plunging** yourself into a **cold** shower on a **long, hot** summer's day?

Those people are happiest who, **regardless** of their **age**, are able to **immerse** themselves in **comic** books.

A good CD played at the right volume at the right time is the perfect medicine for unhappiness.

A good **live** concert in **pleasant** surroundings in the **company** of someone **special** — **that**'s happiness.

A long chat with an old friend makes both of you happy.

After a day in a suit, uniform,
or costume, happiness is
a clean pair of jeans and a
loose pair of slippers.

**A couch isn't a happy
couch until you've
fallen asleep on it.**

Happy days? Driving to buy
fresh almond croissants on
a Sunday morning.

Dancing makes me happy—the extraordinary and compelling life force that leads everyone to feel free enough to shake their entire being in the presence of complete strangers.

The happiest of times are spent reading aloud to someone special at bedtime, or better still, having them read to you.

Going to plays, whether they are good or bad, is an experience that refuels one's faith in human nature.

Singing is to be encouraged, whether you are good at it or not. Happiness is getting in the shower and bawling your lungs out! That is as releasing as it gets.

In a game of charades with friends or strangers, the return to nonverbal communication brings people closer, and everyone is guaranteed a happy time.

Learning the **secret** to a new **magic** trick makes **everyone** happy—**apart** from the trickster.

I am always happy to see craft shops and the infinite possibilities for happiness they provide.

Songs by the **Beatles** sung by those too **young** to have **known** them—that's a **happy phenomenon**.

Revisiting the ponds
where we swam as children
evokes happy memories.

*Happiness to my ears
is finding good acoustics
in the concert hall.*

Three reasons for happiness?
Egg rolling, three-legged races,
and the Indian rope trick.

Reminiscing in the **company** of my **oldest** and **dearest** friends makes for happy **hours** spent **together.**

Eye-catching posters raise a smile.

Happiness is kids' faces hidden behind mountains of cotton candy and sour cherry lollipops and the time to enjoy them.

The **applause** of an audience **fills** my **heart** with **pride** and **happiness**.

Happy hour for me is lying in a hammock slung between two trees, being rocked gently by a cool summer breeze.

The **discovery** of a **bargain** is always a **cause** for **elation**.

The joy of Easter-egg hunts in the garden or anywhere, the excitement of hearing, "You're getting warmer," and then suddenly you see it, all shiny and inviting, an Easter egg in brightly colored foil. That's a child's reason to be happy.

Sitting up talking all through the night with a friend is a magical time.

Some **love** exercising to the point of **exhaustion**. I **prefer** a slice of **chocolate cake**.

I am happy to spend my lunch hour in the park, sharing crumbs with the grateful birds.

Ten minutes in a power shower. Bliss in my own private monsoon.

Dreams and the places they transport me to, up there in the clouds or out on the seas—each new dream is a wonderful adventure.

The happiest place is losing oneself in the flickering flames of an open fire.

Odd perhaps, but there is **no** describing **how** happy I feel when I **listen** to music that **moves** me to tears.

Taking time out to **read** people's biographies is **always** a good **route** to happiness— discovering **inspiration**, or that, surprisingly, we are **not** so different.

A happy sight is a bookcase that is overfilled with inspiring books.

Autumn brings happy occasions like Halloween—people in costumes and fancy-dress parties.

Happiness is composing a symphony and hearing it performed, if only in your head.

To play and just have fun,
forget the competition
and enjoy the game.

When I simply
learned to **relax**,
happiness came
flooding into my **life**
on **all** levels.

When there's happiness in your life
you need never fear boredom.

The sight of a wonderful work of art brings untold happiness.

Happy thoughts attract happiness.

Happy thoughts are formed while soaking in a bathtub full of bubbles.

A happy excursion is had by stumbling upon old songs from the past.

Happiness is the **childlike excitement** of sleeping **rough** on someone's sofa or floor, after a **party** or being **snowed in**.

Here's a happy thought —
I have learned more about life
by laughing at the observations
of the likes of Jackie Mason
and Groucho Marx than I have
from any doctrine that has
been pressed upon me.

The nights when sleep
just **happens** and one
wakes up **refreshed**:
These are to be **celebrated**.

I am always happy to go out of my way to make new friends.

Many people **like** to invest their **time** in the **future**. I am **happier** to spend it with **friends**.

I am happy in the notion of waiting on the river banks with my reel without actually doing it.

A sunny day not wasted will provide
a happy memory to look back on
from the high hill of old age.

*I love happy memories of
boating in the company of
friends, saying nothing,
just gliding along together.*

Happiness is finding the sunshine
of another person's life in a
bottle of the wine they produced.

Lying in bed on a bad-weather day, reading amazing facts, can wash the blues away.

Searching for something special and finding it is definitely a reason to be happy.

Happiness is in the pages of **magical** stories, which, if you were given one **wish**, would never end.

Happiness is a **leisurely** afternoon **browsing** in a library.

Happiness is a lazy day with no have-tos or must-dos.

Happiness is **Dutch courage** at the **top** of a ski run **before** going down it.

Whenever boredom looms, make a spontaneous expedition. That is guaranteed to make you happy.

Happiness is the **delight** one feels on **completing** the **construction** of a sand castle.

And **knocking** it **down**!

Happiness is the **discovery** of an **unused** railway and walking **along** it to discover where it **leads**.

Happiness is unwrapping presents.

Window shopping at festive times, thinking of gifts to give to friends, makes me happy.

Happiness is the thrills and tranquillity of snorkeling in crystal-clear water.

Shadow-puppet shows are about the **most pleasing** and **magical** form on **earth**.

Nothing is more relaxing than just sitting down and watching as the weeds grow round you.

Waving sparklers in the darkness and drawing happy faces in the air—a great way to be happy.

Happiness is the flurry of preparations before a holiday.

Front of house on an opening night is a happy place to be.

Happiness is the anticipation of Christmas.

On the **opposite** end of the see-saw of joyously getting **up** and **out** into the new day is the **bliss** of **sloth**, of taking the **day off** and doing **nothing**.

Rummaging around a bric-a-brac market provides hours of pleasure.

"An intellectual improvement arises from leisure."

SAMUEL JOHNSON

" What is this life if, **full** of **care**, We have no time to **stand** and **stare**?"

W. H. DAVIES

To schoolchildren happiness comes with the end of exams, the arrival of holidays, and the freedom to run and play.

I am happy to announce that I have **never** enrolled in a class in **step** aerobics and my heart is **still** beating happily.

Time for leisure is the true indicator of a civilized society.

Anything penned by Oscar Wilde that can fit into my pocket makes me happy.

The unmistakable **smell** of **brand-new** shoes while standing in an elevator **suggests** that someone among you is **happy** with his **purchase**.

I'm always happy to delve into fiction where the imagination can run wild.

5

Travel and the Wider World

I remember the happy race to take over the backseats on coaches on holiday tours.

I'm glad that man cannot travel any faster on land than he already does.

The thing that's **better** than **getting there** is the **discovery** that you **will** be arriving **on time**.

It makes me happy that one **can** spend an **entire** day collecting **smiles** from strangers—**twice** as **many** when one smiles **first**.

It should make anyone happy to hear anyone else speaking in their native language. It is a sign of freedom and celebration of diversity.

Christmas and Chanukah, Diwali and Ramadhan, Bastille Day and Guy Fawkes night, and all times of celebration for all peoples throughout the world are reason for happiness.

A **happy** smile is always **welcome**, and the **nicest**, it seems, is the **smile** of a **stranger**.

The happiest place to have a cappuccino would have to be Venice.

Happiness is having enough fuel in the gas tank to take off on a drive to the country or an excursion to the city.

I love looking at anything by Monet, preferably at his house! That makes me happy.

Walking happily will get you everywhere!

A trip to an art gallery is like receiving a transfusion of optimism.

Road trips are not for the faint-hearted, but there's adventure and happiness to be had out there beyond the front gate.

"True happiness, we are told, consists in getting out of one's self, but the point is not only to get out; you must stay out; and to stay out you must have some absorbing errand."

HENRY JAMES

I have learned more about life and people's quests for happiness from chats with strangers at bus stops and in airport lounges than from those closest and dearest to me.

Traveling stirs feelings, emotions, and anticipations like no other enterprise. The more unknown the destination, the more powerful the reaction.

If you want to give the impression that you are a happy, determined person then take up cycling.

Happiness is a train when it runs on time.

Happiness is **inspiration gained** from **catching** a **glimpse** of the **birds** as they **fly south** for the winter.

Happiness is turning a corner from a busy city street to discover an oasis: a garden or well-kept window box.

Sitting in a café **window** just **watching** people as they **pass by** is a happy pastime.

Entering **castles** is like entering a **dream**. If you're happy to use a little **imagination** they can soon become **populated** as they may once have been.

Smells that transport me to certain happy times and locations I have known include maple syrup, new-mown hay, cinnamon, and certain French tobacco.

Happy times and happy places include the beach in summer, the woods in fall, the mountains in winter, and the meadows in spring.

The relics of history, museums, and artifacts are great purveyors of delight.

Happiness is discovering your favorite hotels remain unchanged despite the pressures of the years.

If one wants a happy, stress-free excursion, take a pedometer that doesn't work at all.

Happiness is discovering there is free Shakespeare in the park.

"The feeling remains that God is on the journey, too."

St. Teresa of Avila

Go for happy days spent walking, shopping, and having dim sum in Chinatown.

What better reason to be happy than long walks on sandy beaches on misty mornings, hunting for shells and buried treasure?

Happiness is discovering the reemergence of farmers' markets in your locale.

One should always be happy to discover that the light at the end of the tunnel is not a train coming at you from the other direction.

Life is a journey, and to enjoy it, you have to occasionally become a tourist.

There is nothing I could stick on a shelf that could ever compare in value to the memory of a wonderful, happy journey.

"Happiness is like those palaces in fairy tales whose gates are guarded by dragons: We must fight in order to conquer it."

ALEXANDRE DUMAS

Happy are those who by adopting the wisdom of the earth live freely.

We can all seek out ways to preserve the world and, where necessary, be happy to help change the world around for the better.

*Discovering great places
is also about discovering
what makes you happy.*

My life choice is to blend the wisdom
and teachings of the past with the
complex world I live in now. This
provides me with a happy balance
and a positive outlook for the future.

I am grateful that I am happy
to communicate freely with
others at all levels of life.

"I'm now arrived, thanks to the gods!
Thro' pathways rough and muddy."

ROBBIE BURNS

Happiness is my **ability** to **love** and to **embrace** with my love the **space** around me and **all** it **contains**.

Interaction with like-minded but different people is never unpleasant.

The memory of a journey
brings us happiness for
years to come.

If you work and live to serve others
as well as yourself and strive to
leave the world a better place than
you found it, you will have found
a superb reason to be happy.

Thank goodness
I have chosen not to
be unadventurous.

I always **try** and **ensure** that my **surroundings** are **sympathetic** to **happiness**.

"To see a world in a grain
of sand
And heaven in a wild flower,
Hold infinity in the palm
of your hand
And eternity in an hour."

WILLIAM BLAKE

Happiness is digging up history in some ancient field and discovering our links with the past.

Where does happiness reside? Within happiness.

The influence that **one** happy person can have upon the **rest** of the world is **beyond** estimate.

All holidays hold the potential for great happiness!

Listening to the travel tales of seagulls being screeched out for all to hear, from the comfort of a beach towel on a sun-drenched beach, is a happy occupation for several hours.

One can never be happy until it is understood that no journey can begin until one takes the first step.

With happiness there are
only two rules on the path:
Begin and Continue.

Like a **ship**, we can either
remain **tethered** to the **pier**
or happily **set sail** on an
ocean of **discovery**.

The **moon's happy
nature** is the **same** in any
country, in any **language**.

"For my part, I travel not to go anywhere, but to go. I travel for travel's sake. The great affair is to move."

ROBERT LOUIS STEVENSON

For **some** happiness takes the form of bus rides into the **hinterland**, for others a bus ride takes them to **WORK** and back.

Happiness is driving with a clear road ahead.

The discovery of a message in a bottle is most invigorating for the spirit.

Happiness is knowing you can make a fire without matches. Anytime. Anywhere.

The sound of an old Spitfire looping the loop somewhere nearby stirs happy memories and mixed emotions.

Red sails in the sunset make for a happy ending to the perfect day.

If one is not happy to experience the customs of foreign lands, one would be better off remaining at home.

Happiness is taking a moment just to sit back and dwell on the events of the world, releasing a prayer for peace to whoever may be listening.

Happiness is discovering mutual ground despite deep cultural differences.

That peoples of the world have begun to get closer despite the aspirations of despots and dictators is a happy sign for the future.

It is a happy day when great tracts of people around the globe are concerned enough about this world to stand up and be counted.

These days, with e-mail and Internet, even hugs and kisses can be sent virtually all over the world whenever they are needed. They provide instant happiness.

Taxi drivers who know where they're going are a happy breed.

Simulcast concerts that unite the world leave happiness and optimism and the desire to make an effort in their wake.

Tales of adventurous daring are happily received at most any time.

Remember always that you are just a visitor here, a traveler passing through. The secret is to enjoy the journey and leave some happiness behind you for those who will follow.

Considering the actions of each of us, how can anyone be unhappy to coexist?

The discovery of things that inspire us in the outside world ignites happiness within us.

Happy postcards are like little vacations received.

We sometimes have to begin the walk before we're certain of the route. Do so in the spirit of making happy discoveries along the way.

We can all rest assured and find comfort in the fact that there is never nowhere to go.

Other people's **passions** are good reasons for happiness.

A welcoming light in the window at home is a happy beacon to a weary traveler.

The vastness of human potential is good cause for happiness.

Looking for reasons for happiness, we soon discover that it is to be found in the most unlikely places, and rarely in those places where we would have sought it.

Happiness is not the place we seek to get to. It's less the destination and more to do with the way we choose to travel.

Happiness is not being out there in the wilderness with those hunters engaged in the mad, heated pursuit of happiness.

Happiness comes with realizing that some journeys in life are within and have no end.

Happiness is having the ability to remain calm under all circumstances regardless of difficulties or hardships.

Who is unhappy when they know where they are going?

I know where I am going, and that is one of the greatest reasons for happiness there is.

To find happiness, where before you looked at everything with a critical eye, now look for the joy first.

I'm very happy that **skyscrapers** were built **upward** and not **sideways**.

I am happy to know that by using the power of my mind I am free to go anywhere.

"My heart is warm with the
   friends I make,
And better friends I'll not
   be knowing
Yet there isn't a train
   I wouldn't take
No matter where it was going."

EDNA ST. VINCENT MILLAY

Happiness is having
a good chat with a
fellow traveler.

Happiness is bringing home souvenirs that augment my memories.

Happiness is watching videos of past travels and reliving the moment.

Pyramids, geysers, underground cities, and hanging gardens are destinations that make my heart beat faster.

"Slow down and enjoy life. It's not only the scenery you miss by going too fast—you also miss the sense of where you are going and why."

EDDIE CANTOR

To leave my **footprints** on the **wet sand** of every remarkable **beach** to say that I was **there** makes me happy.

Happy **smells** are those that are **not** part of my **everyday** being, but **memorable** scents that **transport** me to another **time** and **place**.

Imagine the happiness felt by African villagers who, until the construction by aid workers of a well, had never before seen water from a tap.

Happy is the **sailor** who **spies** on the **horizon** a **safe** harbor during the **storm**.

Every astronaut that has ever been has brought a warm glow of happiness to my heart.

Happiness is being in any situation that provides one with a sense of freedom.

The return of a loved one after a long absence is cause for happy celebration.

When we open ourselves to the possibility of happiness in our lives then it can be triggered as easily as finding a coin or waking to a sunny day.

There can always be a happy future if we are just prepared to be forgiving.

When you are unhappy, discover the sunshine within by discovering what lies on the other side of the door from where you are standing.

With enough reasons why, you'll always find a way—where there's a way there's happiness.

When happiness **enters** the world, a **wish** comes **true**— **anytime** and **anywhere**.

Any sort of coincidences possess the potential for happiness.

Just **wanting** happiness in our life **lays** the **foundation** for the **path** to happiness.

Never feel ashamed of showing the world how you are feeling.

Life is filled with choices! Happiness is about constant growth and making discoveries about ourselves, others, and the world on a daily basis.

Happy people are those who aren't afraid to be themselves.

Happiness is achieving an understanding that goes beyond language.

People who will keep an open mind provide happiness for themselves and others.

6

Family
and Friends

The recovery of a friend who has been ill is a wonderful reason to be happy.

Reading **letters** from distant **friends** is **always** a pleasure.

People who press flowers and send them to you bring happiness into your life.

Happiness is watching my daughter play hide-and-seek with her cat.

I'm happy to admit that some of my very best friends are trees.

I am glad in the knowledge that I have family and happier still that they do not all live too close to me.

Ask children which they would prefer—to spend more time with their parents, or to have their parents work more to buy them presents and vacations—and they will tell you in no uncertain terms what makes them happy.

"Health is the greatest gift, contentment the greatest wealth, faithfulness the best relationship."

BUDDHA

My uncles are like cartoon characters. They never fill their suits correctly and always speak too loudly, but they do amuse me.

Can anything beat the **gratifying** feeling that comes from **basking** in the **laughter** of my guests at a well-timed **punch line**?

The **only** thing to **compare** with a **conversation** with a complete **stranger** is allowing yourself to **stop** from time to time and **enjoy chatting** to a friendly **cat**.

There is love and there is unconditional love, and I love them both unconditionally.

One can never receive too many hugs.

The only thing better than watching the surprise on someone's face when you give them an unexpected gift is the feeling you get when one arrives for you.

Happiness is being able to shoot the breeze with friends.

Always **there** for me, always to be **trusted**, the **love** of my **friends** brings **happiness** beyond **compare**.

Happiness is having a teddy bear—your own during your childhood, or that of your child. Companions in the dark, they never let you down.

Having my hair brushed brings back happy memories of childhood.

Writing poems makes you **feel good,** but having a poem written **for** you is the **happiest therapy imaginable.**

There is **always** room in **anyone's** life for a little bit of **praise** or a **compliment.** Such happiness they can bring.

The return of fortune to a friend who has been having a difficult time is reason to celebrate.

Here's a happy thought—your happiness can illuminate the happiness of countless others. Don't be stingy, be happy.

"No man can be happy without a friend, nor be sure of his friend till he is unhappy."

THOMAS FULLER

Playing a board game with those closest to you brings happiness all around.

Finding smiles that were meant just for you— especially the sincere ones— makes a person happy.

Happiness is
**reassurance—
good** to both
give and **receive**.

There are big reunions, and
then there are the happy
little reunions at the end of
each school or working day.

What better joy than the
sheer joy of being accepted?

The shock of a new hairstyle on one of my friends makes me happy, so long as they are, too!

Just simply living life in the company of friends and family is cause enough for happiness.

A good reason for being happy would be having my family near.

There are **many** moments to **look forward to** in life, and my **favorites** are the **tender** moments.

Discovering the sensitivity in others that you never knew existed is cause to be happy.

290

"A new friend is like new wine; when it has aged you will drink it with pleasure."

APOCRYPHA ECCLESIASTICUS 9:10

The **unspoken** dedication of pets and the **company** they provide are **happy aspects** of **owning** them.

When two lives connect, happiness illuminates both.

" You are forgiven for your happiness and your successes only if you generously consent to share them."

ALBERT CAMUS

Laughing fits that leave you aching all over are great providers of happiness.

Happiness is the knowledge that this life can be heaven if we give ourselves a chance.

Happiness comes with understanding people.

"Stay, stay at home, my heart, and rest; Home-keeping hearts are happiest."

HENRY WADSWORTH LONGFELLOW

The best sources of happiness are friends and family. Make time for them.

We are happiest when
we are liked.

We are **happy** when we
are **loved**, not **feared**;
when those around us
give way to our **charm**,
not to our **power**.

**Happiness is appreciating
what you have.**

We can attempt to share in the pain of others or strive to let them share in our happiness.

"True friendship is like sound health; the value of it is seldom known until it be lost."

CHARLES CALEB COLTON

"Friendship makes prosperity more brilliant, and lightens adversity by dividing and sharing it."

CICERO

Happiness is about **embracing yourself** and **those** around you, becoming **more accepting** of **yourself** and **others.**

The first time you find the confidence to say what it is you really think and feel, a happy glow runs through you.

The **confidence** to be **who** you **actually are** is the **root** of **happiness**.

By **allowing** happiness to take a **central** place in our life we develop the **capacity** to **share** happiness with others.

"One friend in a lifetime is much; two are many; three are hardly possible."

HENRY ADAMS

In learning to be kind to yourself, you will bring kindness and be gentleness toward others.

Happiness comes through **sharing** your feelings with others, allowing the **genie** out of the **bottle** from time to time.

Emotional energy is after all energy— which is useless until used.

The most comfortable **cushion** against old age is a **memory** filled with happy moments **shared** with friends.

"Friendship is a strong and habitual inclination in two persons to promote the good and happiness of one another."

EUSTACE BUDGELL

All happy people have something in common: good friends.

**Ah, childhood.
I remember being
happy then.**

Life isn't a race. The
only thing worth
winning is the love
and affection of
family and friends.

Being able to help lighten the burden in another person's life—that makes you happy.

There is no greater happiness than knowing we are loved.

304

I cherish all of my relationships with friends and family.

Happiness is never forgetting those who help us to live a happy life—people who encourage us and assist us.

Happiness is learning to understand, not judge, family and friends.

"Between friends there is no need of justice."

ARISTOTLE

Tell yourself, "No one is more fortunate than I."

Happiness is raising a child to be herself.

I am happy that I have opened myself to others and discovered mutual needs in my relationships with others.

Happily I **socialize** more and **open** myself to making **new** friends.

"True happiness is of a retired nature, and an enemy to pomp and noise; it arises, in the first place, from the enjoyment of one's self, and in the next from the friendship and conversation of a few select companions."

JOSEPH ADDISON

Rejoice in the affection shown to you by friends, lovers, and family. Don't be afraid to enjoy it.

When I am a source of kindness and happiness for others I become a recipient of reciprocal kindness and happiness.

"Let us be grateful to people who make us happy; they are the charming gardeners who make our souls blossom."

MARCEL PROUST

Cards from loved ones when I am unwell bring me happiness.

Envelopes that have been **lovingly** decorated in my **honor** are a **great** source of happiness.

Good friends, and just knowing they are there, is a happy comfort.

"Govern a family as you would cook a small fish—very gently."

Photographs of things we have done and all the places we have been bring back happy memories.

Happiness is well achieved with surprises that are designed to please.

Other people's collections make them happy enough to want to share them with you.

Oh happy innocence,
oh happier experience.

The giving and receiving
of e-mails is pleasing enough.
For when they convey good
news or opportunities they
become glorious little packages
of instant happiness.

Now I am happy, having planted
a kiss on your forehead.

Be happy that some people love us the very best way they know how. It's just that it isn't always the way we'd have wished.

The heart is far too sacred a place to keep anything meaningless close to it.

Can there be a happier discovery than the discovery that someone believes in you?

315

Happiness is **ridding** yourself of **enemies** by setting **out** to **make** them your **friends.**

Happy, innocent fun is the passing of very secret, hush-hush letters between parents and their children.

Happiness is **discovering** the **journals** of **those** who went **before** us.

The innocent joy of melting into the arms of someone you love is a reason to be happy.

Knowing that you've got someone who will **listen** to you, no matter what. Isn't **that** a good reason to be happy?

I like arriving home and getting happy messages.

I am happy that I have come to know the life-saving quality of hugs.

Things shared in **common** with those **closest** to you are the things that **make** for a **happy** relationship.

Close ties are important antidotes to unhappiness.

As happy as we might think we are, feeling as one with another person, this would soon change if we were compelled to share in their toothache.

A heart, when dissatisfied, is as prone to hatred as the freed heart is to love and friendship. A happy heart has the freedom of the universe.

My cats seem to be always happy to see me; that makes me happy.

One of the best reasons for being happy would have to be the achievement of selflessness.

We can all find **comfort** in the **whispers** of our dear departed. They appear as the sound of **wind** in the **trees**.

Happy memories of school friends are caught on the wind that blows in my direction.

Happiness is watching the delight of others unwrapping presents.

Happiness is a **two-way** conversation where you **both** hang up with a **smile** on your face.

There is a certain happy thrill to arriving in a far-off land and being greeted by a friendly face when all around you are unfamiliar faces.

Happiness is knowing that no distance can keep people apart when they love and care for each other.

The anger at a breakdown is the essential ingredient for the joy of the repair.

The **sweet** sorrow of being **apart** from **loved** ones for a **short** period of time makes for a **very** happy **reunion**.

Be happy that the arithmetic of love is not without some challenging equations.

We should all be happy in the knowledge that there is always a place to retreat to: one's own solitude.

Happy conversations are the ones that take off on strange tangents.

*What makes me happy?
Just being with you.*

Caution in love is said to be fatal to happiness.

There is great happiness to be gained from supporting others.

The nicest thing any of us could ever say about somebody else is that we don't know what we would have done without them.

I would not be happy to burden other people with all my thoughts, and therefore a journal is a useful way of getting them down for posterity—and for anyone who may wish to look back on them.

Happiness is about **feeling** at **home** and making **others** **feel** at **home**.

Happy are **those** people who **know** what their **little treasures** are in life.

Happiness is following your heart.

When you first witness the glow of happiness on the face of someone you love, the desire will remain with you to awaken that light again and again.

Here's a happy thought: Friends, like fine wine, mellow with age.

I remember the happiness of hours spent playing with childhood friends in the old-fashioned playgrounds we used to have. I simply close my eyes and we're there again.

The very first loving kiss brands a happy memory onto our mind.

Good deeds that remain **anonymous** bring **greater** happiness.

You would be happier in the long run to realize in time that by being too sensitive one can waste an entire life.

Happiness is **preparing** for a **valued** friend who is coming to stay.

Happiness is a great cause for celebration. When you're happy every day becomes a holiday.

Happiness is sending photographs to friends of shared moments.

"My best friend is the man who in wishing me well wishes it for my sake."

ARISTOTLE

Happiness is the heartfelt embrace of a mother.

Happiness for **someone** who is **homeless** may **simply** take the form of **not** being ignored in the street, or the **offer** of a cup of coffee.

Happy is the **orphan** child whom someone **loves** enough to call their **own.**

"The family is the test of freedom; because the family is the only thing that the free man makes for himself and by himself."

G. K. CHESTERTON

Happiness is the **reunion** of refugee families with their **loved** ones following strife. They may have **nothing** they used to own but they have everything in **each other**.

Happiness is the mother who stays calm when a youngster drops the Christmas turkey en route to the table. Making light of the disaster, she sees through the celebration and says, "Never mind darling, let's go and get the other one!"

Happiness is a **coincidence** of **bumping into** an old friend, **stumbling upon** something that brings back a happy memory, **discovering** you have a long-lost twin, or the **first meeting** between grandparents and their grandchildren.

Can anything make anyone happier than having the words, "I love you," whispered in their ear, especially after not hearing it for so very long?

Happiness is redressing your priorities after the realization that while things can be replaced, people cannot.

Happiness is a favorite piece of jewelry that is a special gift from someone you love.

It is possible for anyone to be happy, regardless of the situation they live in, the money they make, or their marital status. Sometimes all it takes is a loving hug or sharing some chocolate.

7

Happiness Among Others

The happiness we get from material things rarely lasts long, and this form of happiness comes and goes.

Good news at any time is welcome here.

"I shall never be so happy as when I was not worth a farthing."

ALEXANDER SELKIRK

Aren't you happy that people still decide to become doctors?

The joy of life is discovering that happiness has not been handed down to us on a plate but that we have succeeded in cooking it up for ourselves.

Aren't you happy that people still decide to become puppeteers?

I'm happy to learn that **among** the wolf pack there are **still** some **genuinely** honest people.

I am happy that the angry may be conquered with love.

I am happy that the miser may be conquered with generosity.

I am happy that the liar may be conquered with truth.

I am happy that the ill-natured person may be conquered with goodness.

"Man needs, for his happiness, not only the enjoyment of this or that, but hope and enterprise and change."

BERTRAND RUSSELL

Belief in **true** happiness **conquers** fear.

We should be happy that people in the main are not put off by the actions of others.

It pleases me that charity doesn't always begin and end in the home.

I am **happy** that the half-filled glass is **still** half-filled with the milk of **human kindness**.

I am happy that **despite** the **freedom** of the **press** there are **some** things written and photographed that will **never reach** the printing presses.

It makes me happy that these days the same building can be used as a church, a mosque, a youth club, for a yoga class, and a crèche.

I am happy in the knowledge that good manners is the preferred path for most, despite all the odds.

That people are **still** making discoveries or **searching** for new ones for **our** benefit makes me **feel** somehow **safer** and **happier**.

I am delighted that, despite the sexual revolution, people still meet and fall in love.

Great happiness is to **help** another person and **never** feel the need to **share** the fact with a **single** soul.

I treat my dealings with other people rather like a friendly game of cards. When the better hand wins, we both find happiness in the outcome, whichever way it goes.

No one's head aches when he is comforting another. All that is felt is happiness.

All the hope and anticipation of a handshake turns to happiness on the giving and receiving of one.

"Different men seek after happiness in different ways and by different means, and so make for themselves different modes of life and forms of government."

ARISTOTLE

Happiness is not always conforming with the world's ways.

Happiness results from simplicity,
and happiness results in simplicity.

It is okay to be **different** if you **allow** yourself to **feel** happy being so. If you do what has **always** been done, you will **only ever** achieve what **is** already there.

Happy are those who are
inspired by love, moved by beauty,
and guided by knowledge.

We **all** have it **within** us to go through life being tender, compassionate, sympathetic, and tolerant. That **should** make us a **bit** happier.

As we **sow**, so shall we **reap**. So it is better to **plant** the seeds of happiness **now** if we **wish** to be happy for the **future**.

The **realization** of happiness can work for **all** of us, no matter **what** our race, culture, religion, lifestyle, or circumstances.

Happiness is the **certainty** in our **own** mind that at **any** time of **our** choosing we **can** rid ourselves of **negative** conditions.

I am happy that I am free to follow my own instincts.

Happiness is knowing that even though we may be by ourselves, we are all in this life together.

"The purpose of our lives is to be happy."

THE FOURTEENTH DALAI LAMA

Happy thoughts come and go
like glimpses of the moon.
When the dark clouds pass
the moon will still be there.

*Have you ever
noticed the immediate
positive and happy
effect of simple
common courtesies?*

There is happiness to be **gained** from **not** working toward **any** goal that might **conflict** with your **values** and **sense** of **purpose**.

The happiest people know that we have only been loaned this wonderful world for the span of our life, and they aim to leave it a better place for the next generation.

We can build a happier world just by making our own happiness a priority in our lives.

A family at peace is a happy sight.

Well-prepared **sermons** by rabbis and priests provide a few **happy** thoughts to **inspire** us to **better** things.

It would make me happy to discover any political party that cared for all nations.

Don't waste time dwelling on the things that annoy you and you'll raise your levels of happiness.

Happy people send and receive harmless brown-paper parcels tied up with string through the mail.

"Happiness, that grand mistress of the ceremonies in the dance of life, impels us through all its mazes and meanderings, but leads none of us by the same route."

CHARLES CALEB COLTON

Each and every one of us has the choice to spend what remains of our life in happiness, even if it is only for a single minute.

Those **less** fortunate than ourselves do **not** need to **hear** about **our** happiness, but we can **help** them to locate their **own**.

When we are happy, the happiness we share with others is the best gift any human being could give another.

No person has the right to let their greed encroach upon the rights and happiness of others.

Why be happy? Because there is no better way to live.

I am **happy** that it is **perfectly** okay to be **admired** and that we have brains **enough** to make **fools** of ourselves. **Sometimes.**

The people who make me happiest are those people who really make you want to listen, and who keep you thinking about what they said for a long time afterward.

Honesty and truth make one happy.

"To live we must conquer incessantly, we must have the courage to be happy."

HENRI FREDERIC AMIEL

Nothing makes me happier than being able to trust someone.

I take my hat off to people who are too busy celebrating life to be unhappy.

Happiness comes from making certain that there is always something to look forward to.

Be happy at anything that gives us the opportunity to celebrate.

Neither shall be happy so long as the wealthy man envies the carefree peasant and the impoverished man envies the idle rich.

Happiness is **theirs** who have good **fortune** and good **sense**.

"The hardest habit of all to break is the terrible habit of happiness."

THEODOSIA GARRISON

Happiness is about being **motivated** to take **positive** steps **daily** to reach **achievable** goals.

Happiness is **offered** by **anything** that is **capable** of **uplifting** humanity with **dignity**.

Happiness is achievable when we learn to accept that there are things in life we cannot change.

"Before we set our hearts too much upon anything, let us examine how happy they are who already possess it."

FRANÇOIS, DUC DE LA ROCHEFOUCAULD

The inspiration that comes from people who have survived difficult times makes one feel glad to be alive.

Happiness is recovering from any form of illness with the support of loved ones.

Man sets out to create the perfect world and in doing so creates a world in which happiness is almost impossible. Yet what remains his deepest wish? To be happy, of course!

Show your happiness and people will see you as you really are.

Happiness is **knowing** the **difference** between **being alive** and being alive **with happiness** in your life.

In our past, we may have been told we don't deserve to be happy. Well, our character is not sculpted out of cold stone. Things change, and everybody has the right to be happy!

To those who fear the past, happiness would be a self-inflicted form of memory loss.

Happy people's lives are **measured** not in **dollars** or **pounds** but in their **simple pleasures**.

Those who are caught up in a quest for happiness while they remain indifferent to the happiness of others will never find their own.

Happiness is the **winged bird** passing us in **flight**, not its **capture** and **incarceration**.

Some people find more happiness in a passing moment than others do in an entire lifetime.

Take a look at happy people and see what it is they are doing: Building a boat and sailing it.

Happiness comes through being and not through having.

If happiness comes as a ray of sunshine in our lives, then we will never be lost in the shadows again.

Happy thoughts: Each has a mind, each mind is its own place, and for some it holds a heaven.

Happiness comes from being part of life and not standing separate from it.

When we feel secure we feel infinitely happier than those people who go through life feeling insecure.

Once we can escape **envy** we can enjoy each **moment** to the **full** and bring **ourselves** into the **sunshine** of our happy life.

Ask yourself this: "Do you believe in true happiness?" If you do, then why not grab it with both hands.

There are **many** varied ways of getting to happiness. All it takes is a little bit of **desire**, a little bit of **guidance**, and a **lifetime** of **practice**.

Understand that happiness won't find us. It is there, always, waiting for us to come to it.

It doesn't take great sacrifices
to achieve a happy life.

Make time to **acknowledge**
and **appreciate** what you
have and you'll **find** that
you have **many** reasons
to be happy.

Happiness is the rubber
stamp of approval.

A world without hunger is happiness.

It is never too late to find happiness. Want it enough, and it will jump right out at the click of your fingers.

Happiness is to **speak** with **freedom** and **free** from **fear.**

"Happiness is the meaning and the purpose of life, the whole aim and end of human existence."

ARISTOTLE

Happiness for one man is a step toward happiness for mankind.

"If all our happiness
is bound up entirely
in our personal
circumstances it is
difficult not to demand
of life more than it
has to give."

BERTRAND RUSSELL

Happiness belongs to those who never wake feeling like a bystander in life.

We can **live** a **happy life** or **waste** an entire **lifetime** waiting for a **single reason** to be **happy**.

People who know what they want are far happier than those lost in the fog of doubt.

383

"Live all you can; it's a mistake not to. It doesn't so much matter what you do in particular, so long as you have your life. If you haven't had that what have you?"

HENRY JAMES

For some there is no particular purpose, cause, or reason for being happy apart from the fact that they just are. That seems a good reason to me.

Change in yourself changes everything in your life. If you want happiness, change.

"It is neither wealth nor splendor, but tranquillity and occupation, which give happiness."

THOMAS JEFFERSON

Endeavor to make your fellow creatures happy— and find happiness.

Having everything will not gain you happiness. Those who are without some of the things they want out of life are by far the happier.

If we were to **wait** always for the **right** reason to be **happy** then we would go through life **never** having **known** happiness **at all**.

Praise from another is always reassuring. It is like having a big okay passed down to you to set you happily on your way along the correct path.

"Happiness always looks small while you hold it in your hands, but let it go, and you learn at once how big and precious it is."

MAXIM GORKY

"Happiness is composed of misfortunes avoided."

ALPHONSE KARR

Imagine the happiness of discovering that you are free after being held captive.

Happiness belongs to the fox that outruns the hounds, the rabbit that avoids the snare.

Happiness is in the eye of the child as it watches the candles flicker on a birthday cake.

To a **youngster** sheer **joy** may be the arrival of a new **garden swing**; to those **older** it may take the form of a **patio chair. Whose** happiness is the **greater**?

Happiness comes with being able to accept our need to share this world with other people and discovering their acceptance of us.

At any given time there are a million reasons or more to feel good and the best way to start is with a smile.

Botox changes the **look** but will not **remove** the **reasons** for **frowning** faces. **Happiness** is the **best** natural **face-lift** there is.

Happy are those who have the attitude that there is enough room in the sunshine for all of us.

"Happy the man whose wish and care
A few paternal acres bound,
Content to breathe his native air,
In his own ground."

ALEXANDER POPE

Happiness is never diminished or diluted by sharing it with others. It is like a flame. One candle may light many others and still burn just as brightly and for just as long.

Happiness is a car that starts no matter how cold it is.

Happiness is a world at peace.

"He who knows enough is enough will always have enough."

LAO TZU

Don't cloud your happiness by feeling compelled to run the whole distance when really you want to run part.

Imagine the **happiness** of a **child** who has **never** had the **opportunity** to attend school, but is **suddenly** given **access** to an education.

Imagine the happiness of the parents who see hope for that child.

Much happiness is missed by going through life unbelieving of anything and everything simply because there is no supporting reason.

Happiness is about finding forgiveness within yourself.

Life is too precious to live it only in your dreams.

Banish self-pity and take a step on that vital path to a happy and satisfied life!

We cannot be happy while we remain dependent upon the material things life sends to distract us—remove the dependence and you will discover happiness.

Happiness is about realizing that our memories, no matter how bad they may seem, are important to us.

Happy, are we not, that we decided that happiness was worth striving for?

The things we **should** all value in life: our **relationships**, our **health**, and our **integrity** — there is **happiness** to be **gained** from **each**.

Happiness is about kindness.

Happiness is about discovering the forgiveness of others toward us.

Happiness is about finding forgiveness within yourself.

My heart is free
of hatred when
I am happy.

*Those who recognize
beauty can discover
happiness at any
moment, in almost
any circumstances.*

The Joy
of Nature

Whenever I feel myself up to my neck in a concrete jungle, I look to nature and take comfort from knowing it belongs to all of us and we to it.

Long walks through the summer grass make me happy.

Welcoming home the **birds** from their **migration** makes me feel happy.

Happiness is the blazing colors of fall.

There's happiness in **stacking firewood** and hoping for a **sudden chill.**

The exhilaration
I feel in the midst
of a thunderstorm
is happiness.

"When you look up at the
sky, you have a feeling of
unity, which delights you
and makes you giddy."

FERDINAND HODLER

Happiness is the **knowledge** that after the **rainstorm sunshine** will follow.

The hush that accompanies snowfall fills me with quiet happiness.

Happiness is looking at the forest floor beneath your feet, piled deep in life, a testimony of time and a chronicle of struggle and achievement.

Despite what we're **constantly** being **told** about this **world**, there are **trillions** of things to be **thankful** for.

There's happiness in the knowledge that, **despite** soya, lambs **still** gambol in the fields in springtime.

Living a life of harmlessness toward all living beings brings happiness all around.

A **walk** on the **beach** on a warm summer night is a **journey** to the **soul** of nature.

Happiness is planting a tree and seeing a forest.

A basket of **fresh** field mushrooms, picked on a **misty** morning, to be consumed in **good** company, makes for a happy **evening** to come.

No one can ever
be miserable who has
mastered the art of
creating a daisy chain.

*There is more
happiness to be
found from loving
all four seasons
than just one.*

I have made a rule for myself that I shall only continue to be happy for as long as the sun rises each morning.

"Adopt the pace of nature."

RALPH WALDO EMERSON

Happiness can be found in **strange** places—watching **earthworms** perform their curious **dances** under the **raindrops,** for example.

There is happiness in the **sound** of the **leaves** **whispering** their **approval** as I **walk** along the pathway that **leads** through the wood.

The day is such fun that the river seems to be giggling along its way.

Take the time to listen to brooks babbling happy secrets from centuries past.

Molehills tell of an entire other world and a desire to make contact.

Stepping-stones are like little birthdays leading to an age of discovery.

There is a happy continuity in the fallen log that still has a use to generation after generation who cross the river upon it.

The explosive takeoffs of woodcocks and pheasants send tingles down the length of my spine.

The view from the top of a mountain on a clear day tells me I am happy and never alone.

Happiness can be found in the inviting colors of a cool fall day.

The rustling of dry leaves in the breeze, each telling the other, "You jump first," is happiness to the ear.

Happiness is the little **Thermos** that my partner gave me, **filled** with piping hot coffee, **enjoyed** from a tree stump at the **head** of the valley.

Mud, glorious mud.
New galoshes and
glorious mud.

Any encounter with nature that makes me feel tiny, makes me happy.

When birds are **outdoing** each other in **coded** song, their **complicated** rhythms make my own **pulse** want to join in.

Happiness is the **understanding** nature of **night**, never **too dark** to scare, **gently** lulling me to sleep.

I smile on hearing the squirrel that lives in my ceiling as he tosses and turns in his bed.

A happy sound—the **quacking** of the **wild mallards** is like **groaning laughter** after a corny joke.

"All of the animals except man know that the principal business of life is to enjoy it."

ANONYMOUS

The nicest aria to be heard is that of the birds at my window when I wake up.

A moment's secret happiness is in the complicity as I glimpse the old red fox darting guiltily away from the direction of Pheasant Wood.

Happiness is being carried on the clouds that scud across a bright blue sky.

Each time I begin to wonder about the meaning of life and my part in it all, I take myself outside and begin counting the stars—it's an absorbing happiness.

I am happy to observe the incomparable beauty of the dragonfly hovering over the surface of a pond.

Shuffling through **piles** of fallen **leaves**, I have that happy **feeling** of being **connected** to the **earth** as I go.

There is no music so wildly jazzy as the splash of a boot in a muddy puddle.

Only **one** thing can **defeat** the **stubborn** nature of the **frozen** earth—the **tenacity** of the **first** spring shoots as they **struggle** through it.

Happiness is feeling soft falling snow against my face, like little cold, wet, lacy handkerchiefs tossed there playfully by winter fairies.

The **generous** nature of **echoes** as they **return** my **calls** from the mountaintop **fills** me with happiness.

"If you take a flower in your hand and really look at it, it's your world for the moment."

GEORGIA O'KEEFE

Sunny days in the middle of cold winters are enough to lift our spirits.

Happiness is to **acknowledge** that a **walk** is **never** just a walk; it is an **adventure**.

Feel **happy** in the **warmth** of the **sun**. It is like **no** other. It is as if the world's **creator** was **embracing** you in a loving **hug**.

The stars in a clear sky always make me wonder if out there somewhere, someone is looking back at me with equal wonder.

The moon makes me smile. Have you ever seen an unhappy moon? Smile back from time to time.

Once you have **experienced** it you can never forget the **ocean**. Close your **eyes** and you can **instantly** conjure the **sound**, **scent**, and **sight** of it.

Happiness lies with water lilies, on canvas or floating on the pond.

Happiness is watching the courtship dance of the lyrebird as it sweeps fantastic patterns of twigs and broken colored glass.

There is **nothing** as happy making as the **arrival** of the color **green** after months of **brown** naked branches.

Happiness is a lazy Sunday morning filled with the smell of freshly mown grass.

The **wild** unstructured form of **birdsong** fills my **heart** with happiness.

Watching the Virginia creeper change color in tune with the season is a happy sight.

The incredible blue of a field of cornflowers takes my breath away.

Stand back and enjoy the high-colored blowziness of a bed of dahlias.

I am happy contemplating the curious nature of clouds and their persistent attempts to resemble other things.

Catching sight of a **shooting star** fills me with **indescribable** happiness.

I am happy in the company of the wind when it blows through my hair.

Any **tree** that has **survived** man's **appetite** for **timber** is a happy thought.

Happiness is thinking about the giant oaks, the massive red pines, or the sacred banyans where children and monkeys gather and where the Buddha attained enlightenment.

I love the smell of the damp waking earth that signals the arrival of springtime.

The natural **prettiness** of
a **basket** of **primroses**
is a **happy** sight.

**No night is empty
when it is starlit.**

The **tickle** of a **raindrop**
as it **runs** down my **nose**
makes me happy.

There's **excited** happiness in the **discovery** of a **fossil** and the **link** it **provides** with the long-distant **past**.

"One of the pleasantest things in the world is going on a journey; but I like to go by myself. I can enjoy society in a room; but out-of-doors, nature is company enough for me."

WILLIAM HAZLITT

Enough snow having fallen
to embark upon a sleigh ride
and a good hill nearby are
ingredients for a happy day.

*Happiness is the
shimmer of the
golden carp beneath
the sun-filled
surface of the pond.*

Happiness is the discovery of a stone that talks to you.

A happy thought is the possibility of angels looking over me and fairies at the foot of the garden.

No matter how many times you've seen it before, there is sheer magic in watching snow as it falls outside your window.

Enjoy the happy **reaction** of a **puppy** seeing a **snowfall** for the **very first time**.

There's happiness in the **salty smile** forced onto your face by a stiff **ocean breeze**.

Happiness is a dark night dusted with stars.

Pleasure stirs at the sound of a bicycle bell on a country lane.

Happiness comes from discovering that beauty is everywhere and not just in the way people or things look.

There is a **beguiling happiness** in the **beckoning** nature of **mountains.**

Any natural sounds that reach my ears in the morning, before the mechanical sounds of the day encroach, are reasons to be happy.

I love the sound of rain upon corrugated iron.

Any sighting of butterflies is a welcome moment.

Finding flowers in places one wouldn't expect to see them makes me happy.

Learning to love the wind and the rain is a reason for happiness.

There's **happiness** in the **knowledge** that **success** can be **measured** by how we live in **harmony** with the **earth**.

Accepting that there will **always** be things to **discover** about our **earth** and this **universe** is a happy thought.

A quiet landscape that invites me into its presence makes me happy.

When we become at **one** with nature we have **all** the **power** of nature at our **disposal**.

There is happiness to be had by making our fellow creatures happy.

Happiness **comes** from **knowing** that the **meek** shall **inherit** the **earth**.

The simple things in life are like flowers, and happiness is the nectar waiting for you to extract it.

Why seek happiness in the **distance** when it is growing right here at your **feet**?

Happiness is **sliding down** the **colored bands** of **rainbows**.

The sound of **whales** singing is happiness **filled** with **awe**.

Happiness is finding a piece of driftwood that imposes itself on my imagination.

Walking in the **rain** when it's **warm** **envelops** me in a **quiet** happiness.

Happiness is discovering a cluster of ladybugs on the first growth of spring.

Happiness is finding a language in which to commune with the great outdoors.

Happiness is the grin of the harvest moon, all shiny and Buddha-like up there, as if saying to me personally, "I told you it was good!"

The only thing better than a bright, frosty day is feeling warm on a bright, frosty day.

I am happy to receive the frosty kisses that the breeze plants on my cheeks each morning in winter.

When I think of purity and the potential of man in his relationship to all of nature my mind turns immediately to the Dalai Lama.

Happiness is celebrating the infinite qualities of rain, from drizzle to downpour.

Happiness is the **curious look** that **deer** give you just **before** they **dart away**.

Happiness is watching the sleepy hibernation of a hedgehog.

Happiness is going **out of one's way** to take in the cherry blossoms.

Herald some happiness with the arrival of a new season.

Happiness is in the **detail** of **creation** — a leaf **skeleton** or spider's **web**.

Happiness comes by ensuring that we create opportunities that allow us to become at one with nature.

Recognizing that we **all** have a natural wisdom **born** into us is a **happy** thought.

The colors of summer harvest are so deep and rich, you feel you could smell and taste them.

Happiness is a **sunset** that **paints** the sky until everything under it **glows** for miles around.

A happy sweep of wind that tries to lift you off your feet is guaranteed to put a smile on your face.

The crashing sound of waves on the shore and the sound they make as they drag the pebbles back with each retreat makes for happy listening.

Man is part of nature: Happiness will return the instant you start to listen to it.

There's a happy smell of smoke calling to me from the bonfire.

Dispel your **fears,** lie in the **long** grass, and **listen** to the **happy hum** of bees.

There's a thrilling happiness in the foreboding warning of what's to come before a storm.

Feel those happy strokes of the grass on your bare feet.

"A flower falls, even though we love it; and a weed grows, even though we do not love it."

DOGEN

Any form of miracle makes me happy.

Here's a happy thought—
by widening our circle of
compassion we free ourselves
to embrace all living creatures
and all of nature in its glory.

A penful of piglets and a basketful of kittens and chicks is a happy sight.

Remembering those **bucketfuls** of **tadpoles** that become **chattering frogs** makes me happy.

Technology has taken man so far from life, the earth, and nature that he can no longer see that tranquillity and happiness are waiting just outside his door in the fresh air.

Happiness is the belief in the universal **oneness** of **being**: that I am **part** of **everything** and **everything** is **part** of me, and that I have **always been** and **always will be.**

Those who experience the spirituality of nature have awakened in them a deep and satisfying happiness.

Happiness is being able to walk away from any form of natural disaster and still love nature.

To the **fledgling** happiness is **discovering** the **freedom** of **flight** with **loops** and **swoops** and **happy landings**.

Happy is the animal who is **not** tormented but instead treated with **loving** care and **equal** respect as a **creation**, just like **us**, of something **greater** than we may **ever** come to understand.

Published by MQ Publications Limited
12 The Ivories
6–8 Northampton Street
London, N1 2HY
email: mqpublications.com
website: www.mqpublications.com

Editor: Karen Ball
Design concept: Balley Design Associates
Design: Philippa Jarvis

ISBN: 1-84072-548-6

10 9 8 7 6 5 4 3 2 1

Printed and bound in China